II021126?

Interactive Press

Timelord Dreaming

Winner of the Western Australia Premier's Award for Digital Narrative and the Queensland Premier's Award for Poetry among other distinctions, David P Reiter has been recognised internationally for his ground-breaking creative works.

Hemingway in Spain and *Nullarbor Song Cycle* began as text works and later were extended to films. *My Planets: a fictive Memoir* as well began as a physical book and an enhanced CD but then, in collaboration with the Banff Centre for the Arts in Canada, became the innovative *My Planets Reunion Memoir* <http://ipoz. biz/myplanets>, an interactive website in which text, film, audio performances, classical music, astronomy, and animation converge on a journey from separation to reunion of biological families.

In his latest hybrid work, David creates 'tweetems' – text and social media moments – that immerse the reader/viewer in the timeless and sometimes surreal experiences of being an emergency and post-op patient.

Dr Reiter is Publisher/CEO at IP (Interactive Publications) and lives in Brisbane with his wife, two children, and menagerie of irreverent pets.

Interactive Press
Literature Series

Timelord Dreaming:
tweetems from ward 8b

David P Reiter

Interactive Press

Interactive Press
an imprint of IP (Interactive Publications Pty Ltd)
Treetop Studio • 9 Kuhler Court
Carindale, Queensland, Australia 4152
sales@ipoz.biz
ipoz.biz/IP/IP.htm

Printed in 12 pt Cochin on 14 pt Helvetica Neue.

National Library of Australia Cataloguing-in-Publication data:

Author:	Reiter, David P (David Philip), author.
Title:	Timelord dreaming : tweetems from ward 8b / David P. Reiter.
Publisher:	Carindale, Qld. : Interactive Publications, 2015.
ISBN:	9781925231021 (paperback)
Subjects:	Hospital care--Poetry.
	Microblogs.
	Instant messaging.
Dewey Number:	A821.3

for 'Dr Who' and the other dedicated staff at the Mater Hospital, Brisbane, who left me short of one gangrenous gallbladder but well on the road to recovery.

Acknowledgements

This work relies the the sharing of other work that is freely accessible on the Internet and acknowledges its sources via URLs provided in hypertext and footnotes. The author expresses his gratitude to the authors and artists of those referenced artworks and hopes that the counterpoint of those with this will give rise to new appreciative audiences for everyone.

Hospital stays are usually the stuff of clichés. If you're lucky enough to survive your stay in Emergency and get admitted for observation or an operation, and are public enough about your situation, people will take note and chat with and about you. Social media makes it so much easier to document your journey from arrival to departure and points beyond, and for people to share your experiences. Often these will be friends or close acquaintances, but sometimes they'll be "friends" you've admitted to your network for whatever reason who identify with your circumstances enough to message you for all to see.

As a patient, you feel your identity slipping away the longer you remain in hospital. And the older you are, the more likely you'll be called 'love' or 'dear' by time-poor nurses and orderlies. In the artificial light and the drip-haze of medication, time and the senses blur and surreality takes hold. The mind tries to latch onto fragments of the familiar and even these dissolve without a drug free effort to capture them.

I decided to invent a new form to recreate and reflect on these fragments, what I call the *tweetem*. It's a cross between Japanese forms like the tanka and the character-limited tweet. Each tweetem must be self-contained, with a kick in the tail at the end, in 140 characters or less. Whether or not this new form endures, or is even tolerated from the beginning to the ending of the work at hand is up to you.

The overall narrative is under compression, as I've said, but it has the kinetic potential to expand associatively if you pursue the many hyperlinks (diversions) offered. This is easier if you're viewing the digital version but still rewarding if you've opted for the physical book and have an Internet device at hand.

And, yes, the Timelord I met in the haze and half-light *was* real, and I trust that he will one day sidestep out of his parallel universe long enough to meet his more infamous *other*.

– David P Reiter

Contents

Timelord Dreaming:

tweetems from ward 8b

999.1

Ticking boxes: 'is he still conscious?
When did his [1]#chest pains, shortness of breath, begin?
Please secure all dogs & attack guinea pigs.'

---

[1] http://tinyurl.com/koyghox

999.2

In situ: 'you say your father died of a [2]#heart attack?
Have *you* ever smoked?' *Passive* counts.
As my pain tightens… [3]#regeneration coming on?

---

[2] http://youtu.be/sC2nElyx7Ds
[3] http://youtu.be/BehwuPQm16A

999.3

'Please scale your [4]#pain from 1 to 10.
We sustain for the EW – no exits on our watch.
Name, date of birth, allergies – best to *memorise*.'

999.4

Drugs, glorious drugs! *please Mr Para may I have some more?* Mr [5]#Morphine and I have never played tag, until now…

---

[5] http://tinyurl.com/kxel726

4D PRINT FROM THE [6]#TARDIS

[7]#Dr Who at the EW shapeshifts for the transfer, blue jab in my bowels, [8]#centrifuge of max focus betrayed by a tease of dancing lights.

---

[6] http://tinyurl.com/mrrdfyt

[7] http://tinyurl.com/olxvwz8

[8] https://twitter.com/centrifugemusic

'WORSE THAN CHILDBIRTH'

Meanwhile, my wife's FB contacts reassure:
[9]#survivors earn points for deconstructing pain.
As mine edges from constant to intense.

---

[9] http://tinyurl.com/nkv57mq

EW – SUNDAY, MIDNIGHT

'Excluded your heart. Now for the shadows.
My [10]#sonic screwdriver will scan for [11]#aliens.'
Yes, my pain is there, and *there* – a solid 8.

[10] http://youtu.be/LXliD189bss
[11] http://tinyurl.com/kowam3n

SO TWENTIETH C ULTRA

Jellied ball kneading (not even in 3D!)
U-turns that drone over wallflower organs,
pauses verballing the [12]#gallbladder.

---

[12] http://tinyurl.com/k6ujsuy

BLOOD SECRET BUSINESS

Need to know? Even in theatre, privacy comes first.
Tubes, needles, incisions deal out their clichés.
Somewhere, your [13]#<u>universal donor</u> sighs.

---

[14]#DΛLEK LOCK-ON – MONDΛY, 01:00HRS

You are now locked on to our sensors.
Your frail flesh and synapses *will* obey.
Have you scrubbed for your [15]#gods?

---

[14] http://tinyurl.com/klr39mx
[15] http://tinyurl.com/og6c4qe

THE WATCHTOWER – 04:00

Stainless [16]#CareFusion tattles in my stats
throbbing red at each flow dip or interrupt –
I grapple for the green pulse of a call button

[16] http://tinyurl.com/pbe2l9k

DR WHO TO ULTRA – 07:30

Fresh from janitor skin at Clara's school
Dr Who hushes me with a aging finger –
[17]#Mercury, not [18]#Charon, tonight for my tests

[17] http://wordinfo.info/unit/3814/ip:6/il:M
[18] http://tinyurl.com/psqzeym

GOOGLE MAPS FROM JELLY – 07:45

Body mass a [19]#moonscape yielding minerals
to a [20]#footloose scanner, probing for a *presence*
not absence, what will he find? *please* find?

---

[19] http://tinyurl.com/c6qb3js
[20] http://youtu.be/XrqrpMFxMo8

DO NOT PASS GO

I'm admitted to Ward with no roll of dice
surrendering all chances for [21]#Free Parking
As morphine taunts [22]#ghosts from my eyes

[21] http://tinyurl.com/lxn6tnw
[22] http://tinyurl.com/pv8bj62

FEVERSPIKES

Heat shell of [23]#normalcy, atmosphere buffers
our fleshy bits against intruding rays, before
the frantic sorties of [24]#white cell scouts

---

[23] http://tinyurl.com/pagfuue
[24] http://tinyurl.com/n5n47cx

MY [25]#ENDONE GODDESS

Detours from a plastic cup, minimalist,
slightly sweaty in off-white coatings
to sleep [26]#perchance to nightmare … of you

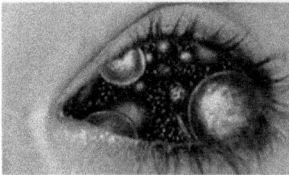

[25] https://twitter.com/queenoftrap
[26] http://tinyurl.com/k83hknb

DAY NURSE 1

'Can you tell me your name, DOB,
known [27]#allergies (cats, dust, pollens)
This needle's not just for *anyone*'

NIGHT WATCHTOWER

I've orchestrated the steady drip-drip
[28]#calibrated to the microsecond
when its mission descant must stop

---

[28] http://youtu.be/g4TDFzEkt9I

I CLOSE MY EYES

And intuit for the position of least
sore on this ripple of bed, waiting
for the latest refrain of [29]#Cybermen

[29] http://tinyurl.com/l63ao8u

DAY NURSE 2

'Can you tell me your name, DOB,
known allergies (cats, [30]#<u>dust</u>, pollens)
These pills are not just for *anyone*'

---

[30] http://tinyurl.com/nnffkfn

THE MIND RECOILS

Invest in flesh and you'll miss the peak
Without [31]#spirit no matter can persist
#brainwaves[32] hustled to the grave

[31] http://tinyurl.com/k2cpbbl
[32] https://www.tumblr.com/tagged/brainwaves

NIL BY MOUTH

Impolite to refuse what isn't offered?
Food & drink will spoil your X-ray [33]#selfie
So let's hector the mystery a while yet

---

[33] http://tinyurl.com/md5bzwy

STATE OF PLAY – 10:05

[34]#Ultrasound: *something's in there*
X-Ray: *50ml fluid on the right lung*
Bloods: [35]#recalcitrant *kidney & liver*

---

[34] http://tinyurl.com/m86bxpu
[35] http://quitegoodcomics.com/

SPARE NO EXPENSE

Dr Who beams with news: a [36]#CT Scan
the final arbiter of organs, top Japanese
[37]#pedigree, no closet for pain to hide

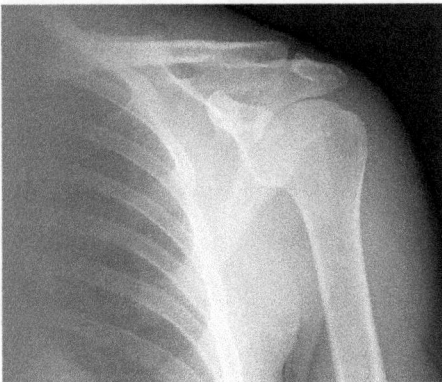

---

[36] http://www.xrayrisk.com/
[37] http://tinyurl.com/o2koyal

[38]#HOLDING PATTERN

Burning off fuel as my bed orbits
I have this [39]#premonition of flames
as surplus-to-requirement credit

---

[38] http://youtu.be/Z1LW3Oq-P7w
[39] http://tinyurl.com/kd69xgm

THIN [40]#RED LASER

Is your ally, so *relax*, sip the air
until safely inside its whirring batcave
Your cells [41]#gently deconstructed

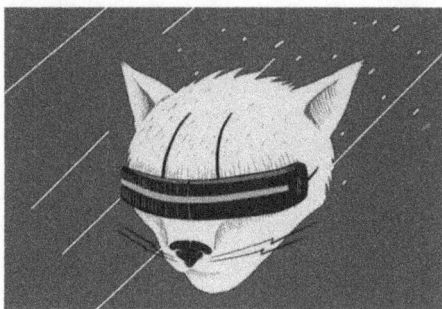

---

[40] http://youtu.be/269BLY_gJ74
[41] http://tinyurl.com/k5f8etb

AND THE WINNER IS

'It's a *nasty*' the senior doctor intones
as his [42]#disciples freeze in mid-note
'[43]#gallbladder', the scribble dissolved

[42] http://tinyurl.com/mqxrrgg
[43] http://tinyurl.com/kqusuq6

A [44]#BETTING MAN

Contemplate your odds: 1 in 300 die
from this op, or is it 299 *live*
to sip from their [45]#glass half-full.

---

[44] http://tinyurl.com/ophkl6l
[45] http://tinyurl.com/k3vtv5f

UNDERSTATED [46]#ACCESS CHANNEL

X marks the [47]#bellybutton, then just under
the breastbone, then two more – 5cm apart
to midriff – that's all we need to cut, excise

---

[46] http://tinyurl.com/oj7vdrd
[47] http://tinyurl.com/m7wehaw

UNLESS

The [48]#unexpected demands a longer slit
to redoubt: he who scalpels and runs away
shall live to [49]#incite another day at better odds

---

[48] http://tinyurl.com/muudmnq
[49] http://tinyurl.com/oms86c2

SIGN HERE

Armed with a laser pen, Dr Who intones
[50]#free will is crippled after this dotted line
To Be or Not, drained of [51]#metaphysical

[50] http://youtu.be/_dE4YrrAAGk
[51] http://tinyurl.com/nrt3bpg

STRINGS THAT UNBIND

No wife, no children, no past, no present
no PhDs, no metonym for [52]#atonement
will express-track you to certainty

---

[52] http://tinyurl.com/qa7cj84

"CRACK YOUR CHEEKS..."

I ponder what [53]#Lear must have felt
forsaken by daughters on that icy heath
but then a warm blanket for my countdown

---

[53] http://tinyurl.com/m5wrsmu

10... 9... 8...

I never
got
that f—

DREAM OPTION I

Ice-blue eyes of wolf, licking lips
against the [54]#whiteout, no bootprint
of death against the [55]#tabula of tundra

---

[54] http://youtu.be/TRCFiJJbKC8
[55] http://tinyurl.com/o9h6h76

DREAM OPTION 2

[56]#

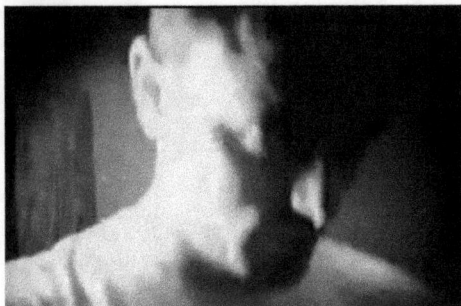

---

[56] http://youtu.be/CHK5animNZY

DREAM OPTION 3

[57]#HeavensGate thanks you for your patience
A verified [58]#angel will be with you shortly
Quote your CRN to unpair the muzak

---

[57] http://tinyurl.com/k37yp77
[58] http://tinyurl.com/nx5aqeo

[59]#SHORT-TERM LOSS

I don't remember: the tube slithering
down my throat, the interrogations,
snips, bleed, metal plug, seal, [60]#curtain call

---

[59] http://tinyurl.com/mxo7u9a
[60] http://youtu.be/SLbuUQ-RNGg

NIGHT NURSE 1

'Can you tell me your name, DOB
known allergies (cats, dust, [61]#pollens)
This needle's not just for *anyone*'

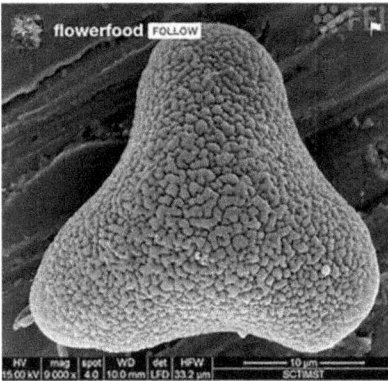

---

[61]https://www.tumblr.com/tagged/pollens

LIKE CANDY

Do I yearn for flirty white pills?
I've scored a [62]#Get Out of Pain Free
to [63]#mute my first overnight

WHITE BREAD AT DAWN

A sure signature of [64]#resurrection
with butter, strawberry jam and tea
Rolled oats waits for no tongue

---

[64] http://tinyurl.com/lz4cpvn

DAY NURSE 1

'Can you tell me your name, DOB
known allergies (cats, dust, pollens)
… and why your [65]#<u>blood oxygen</u> is so low?

---

[65] http://tinyurl.com/ophnjwq

INVOLUNTARY THINGS

We breathe, we are – [66]#auto-pilot is all
our lungs have ever known or need to know
So why sub them with *thought tubes*?

66 http://tinyurl.com/o5cm2x5

LITTLE SURPRISES

Specialist hardens into focus, junior doctors
at heel. 'In the nick of time,' he says, fatherly,
'your gallbladder was [67]#gangrenous!'

---

[67] http://tinyurl.com/qeb2bkz

SHUFFLE THE DECK AGAIN

If 30% of [68]#laparoscopic cholecystectomy patients
with gangrenous gallbladders must convert
to open cholecystectomy, how many draw a [69]#Joker?

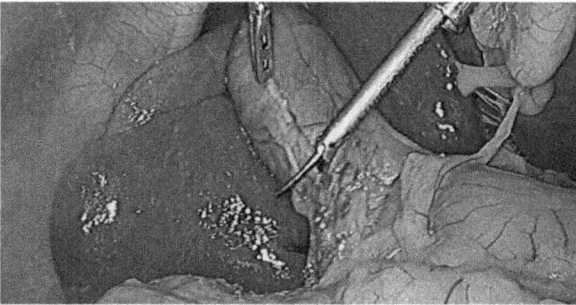

---

[68] http://tinyurl.com/k5pjn28
[69] http://tinyurl.com/l6sxm6j

DVT AND OTHER DISTRACTIONS

'Just a slight sting to thin the blood
until you can get out of bed' chapters
the [70]#no-fly zone between supper and dawn

---

[70] http://youtu.be/68MKyiT3Rro

WHO IS THE FAIREST

Not a [71]#rock star magnet for millions
of likes but my post-op still prompts
more chatter than my latest [72]#Amazon

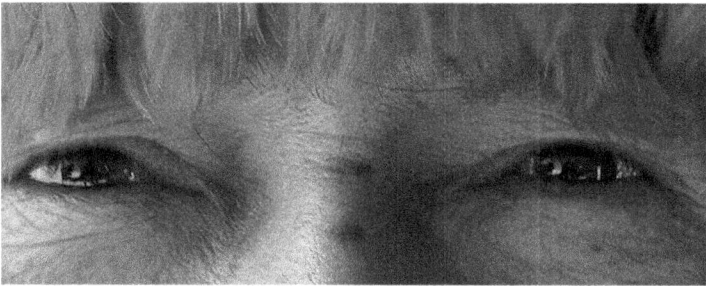

---

[71] http://tinyurl.com/kfkr8a2
[72] https://twitter.com/amazonwatch

IN STATE

Bed 45 is vacant, pristine. 46 is riveted eyes
whenever my curtain is swept back (seldom)
48 is in vacuo, [73]#guesswork between tests

---

[73] http://tinyurl.com/q2tfts5

VEGIE OPTIONS

Your secret is safe with us whisper the beans
coveting the lamb stew's sector, while
poor [74]#omelette shies from the pepper

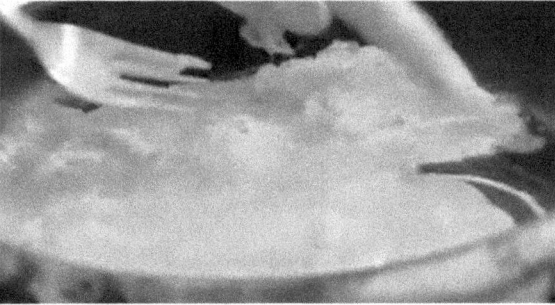

SECRET PATIENT'S BUSINESS

Dismiss any sharp pain as wind
Excuse your implacable bowels
Forgive any thoughts of [75]#mortality

WHO NEEDS PAY TV

In the arterial twilight of the corridor
Dr Who deploys a [76]#maximalist script
[77]#denying his lust for spunky Clara

---

[76] http://tinyurl.com/nd4k87r
[77] http://tinyurl.com/9fkyrx

AS IF YOU'RE NOT HERE

Your sweat has soaked the sheets
but you're shivering to the cliff-edge
of [78]#exhaustion, green button ghosted

---

[78] http://tinyurl.com/mwjczla

NIGHT NURSE 1

'Can you tell me your name, DOB
known allergies (cats, dust, pollens)
Swap for [79]#dry gown? not a problem!'

[79] http://youtu.be/18ij9ubCEM4

A POEM IN IT

[80]#Nil by mouth, nil by page, nil by life
– no inmate roadblocks to reflection –
dreamscapes transition to parole

---

[80] http://tinyurl.com/m4v32dr

'WELL-ORGANISED' SWELLINGS

Never second-guess your [81]#leucocytes
They live for the thrill of surround
and negation of all [82]#nano threats

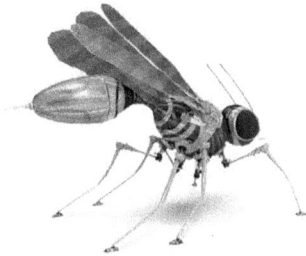

---
[81] https://www.tumblr.com/tagged/leucocytes
[82] http://tinyurl.com/leumm3m

BREATHLESS

My [83]#Incentive Spirometer is [84]#counter-intuitive:
inhale to blow three coloured balls spaceward
red, easy; orange, maybe; black, stubborn

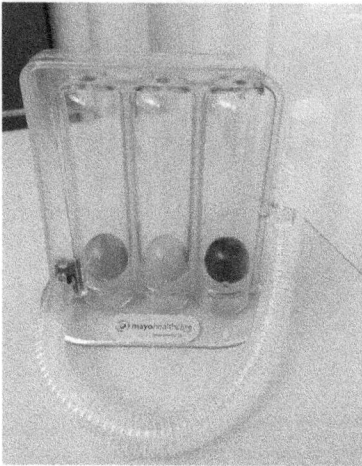

---

[83] http://tinyurl.com/jw4388s
[84] http://tinyurl.com/khantpa

SPLENDID SOLITARY

One faecal test was all it took
to unmask a selfie [85]#superbug
consigning me to a private cell

LONELY WHITE BREAD

[86]#Something there is about a solitary
slice on an immaculate white plate
begging for a slur of strawberry

---

[86] http://tinyurl.com/yvsjey

PAROLE

In this [87]#parallel universe of filtered air
your sense of exit is conflicted by choice
What's our [88]#code white for street clothes?

---

[87] http://tinyurl.com/ltvasc3
[88] http://youtu.be/xSGOSwhzibw

NEGATIVE INCREMENTS

Superstition says *don't ask* for release
Pride comes before a [89]#relapse
and the specialist of course knows best

---

[89] https://vine.co/tags/TheRelapseSymphony

OF A CERTAIN AGE

When your sparks per second have fizzled
and your steps to [90]#recovery stumble
your mind must transfuse patience into will

---

[90] http://tinyurl.com/mrayesx

TARDIS AWAITS

At the [91]#cavalier flash of my medicare card
the crosshairs refresh for a grayscale landing pad
as Dr Who teleports into a new episode

---

[91] vimeo.com/78293068

GRAVITY

If scabs are your only [92]#parachute
plan your [93]#identity removal with care
or your dreams will weep with acid

---

[92] https://www.tumblr.com/tagged/parachute
[93] http://tinyurl.com/ow8e2g6

CATCHING BREATH

Is this how it is at the [94]#edge of space
when Disney blue meets anarchy
black, casting for a slice of [95]#infinity?

---

[94] http://tinyurl.com/mzkrrnt
[95] http://tinyurl.com/kuxvf5y

POST-OP REMIX

Your veins have a trigger for [96]#double-dissolution
after this breach of privacy however faint
across your pockmarked Manus of skin

---

[96] http://tinyurl.com/ktaohzg

SON OVERTAKES

That footprint instant when [97]#age surrenders
to determination, as slight hills steepen
at your now chartable decline

FOREIGN OBJECTS

So the ghost of my gallbladder is sealed
with a [98]#titanium clip, just the right size
to [99]#prevent migration and dribbles of bile

[98] http://youtu.be/JRfuAukYTKg
[99] http://tinyurl.com/lv2966r

HARMONIC OBJECTS

Given my druthers, I'd have chosen a slice
via [100]#Harmonic Scalpel, which seals
as it dissects with shuffled, sterile iTunes.

---

[100] http://tinyurl.com/kgm5xx7

POST-OP BLUES 1

The [101]#small print, unread between the lines
stray sharp twinges, tag-matching the runs
with bloated full-stops, and a pill for each

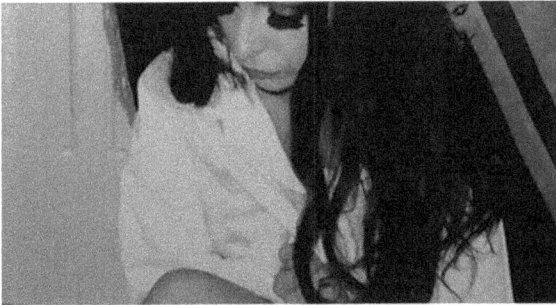

---

[101] http://tinyurl.com/qx3hl9q

POST-OP 2

You memorise the symptoms sheet
at a slant, [102]#Hypochondria Isn't You
– recant all pain for freedom's sake

DR WHO, SKATES ON

Between night shifts, he films an #[103]Arctic
episode with ironic glances at Camera 1
I share – *get on with it, mate, Life that is*

---

[103] http://tinyurl.com/kwjdlo5

MY PARALLEL UNIVERSE

Before: a shard of bronzed immortality
After: an epiphany at my [104]#<u>instant of thaw</u>
Synchronies aligned to a discord of time

[104] https://soundcloud.com/lilocean/falls-x-lil-ocean-thaw